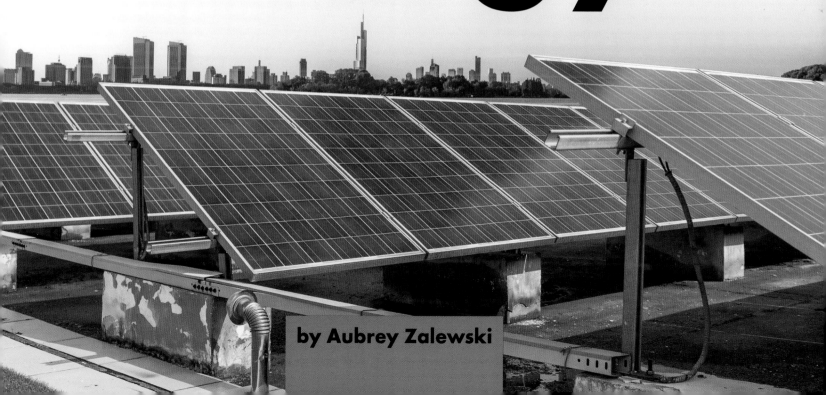

# Renewable Energy vs. Nonrenewable Energy

vs.

by Aubrey Zalewski

**The Child's World®**
childsworld.com

Published by The Child's World®
1980 Lookout Drive • Mankato, MN 56003-1705
800-599-READ • www.childsworld.com

Photographs ©: iStockphoto, cover, 1, 11; Creativa
Images/Shutterstock Images, 5; Andrei Stanescu/
iStockphoto, 6; Shutterstock Images, 9, 12, 15,
16, 19; Zhu Difeng/Shutterstock Images, 20

ISBN 9781503844421 (Reinforced Library Binding)
ISBN 9781503846661 (Portable Document Format)
ISBN 9781503847859 (Online Multi-user eBook)
LCCN 2019956650

Printed in the United States of America

## About the Author

Aubrey Zalewski edits and writes children's books. Aubrey spends her free time enjoying nature, baking goodies, and reading books. Aubrey lives in Minneapolis, Minnesota, with her husband and pet rabbit.

# TABLE of CONTENTS

# CHAPTER ONE

# What Is Energy?

Energy flows through Emmy's life. **Electricity** runs many of the things Emmy uses each day. Electricity is a type of energy. Emmy turns on the light. The light uses energy. Her mother gets eggs from the refrigerator. The refrigerator uses energy to keep the eggs cold. Her mother cooks the eggs. The stove uses energy to cook food. Emmy gets in the car to go to school. The car uses energy. There is a tank full of gas in the car. The car burns the gas. This creates energy to move the car forward. Where does all of this energy come from?

A stove uses energy to cook food.

A car cannot move without using energy.

Energy is the ability to do work. It can cook an egg. It can light a room. It can move the tires on a car. Energy cannot be created or destroyed. It always exists. But it can change.

There are many forms of energy. Heat, light, and electricity are all types of energy. Energy can change forms. Electricity powers a light bulb. The light turns on. The electric energy changed to light energy. Phones, cars, plants, and people all use energy every day.

Energy has to come from energy sources. But people cannot always use the energy directly from these sources. So they change the energy into different forms. These forms carry energy. Electricity is an example of an energy carrier. People can easily use electricity to power many different things.

There are two types of energy sources. One is nonrenewable energy. Energy from this source can be used up. It is not easily replaced. The second type is renewable energy. This kind of energy does not run out. It is easily replaced.

Electricity carries energy to different objects such as light bulbs.

# CHAPTER TWO

# Nonrenewable Energy

Buildings need energy to heat them in cold weather. Many use natural gas. Airplanes need energy to fly through the air. They use fuel that comes from oil. Power plants create electricity. The power plants change energy from one source into electricity. Many power plants use coal as their source. They burn the coal to create steam. The steam pushes a turbine. This movement creates electricity.

Natural gas, oil, and coal are all nonrenewable energy sources. This means that the sources can run out. Once they run out, it takes millions of years to recreate them.

Gasoline is used to power most cars. It is made from oil.

# How Fossil Fuels Form

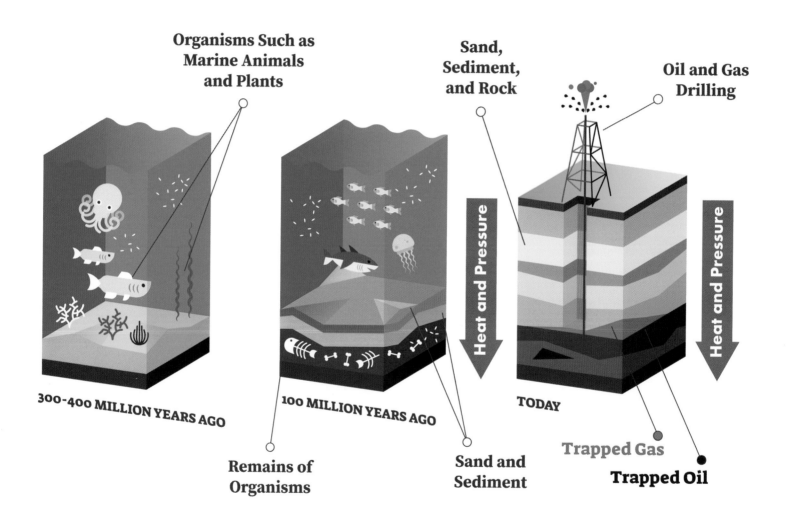

Organisms Such as Marine Animals and Plants

Sand, Sediment, and Rock

Oil and Gas Drilling

Heat and Pressure

Heat and Pressure

300-400 MILLION YEARS AGO

100 MILLION YEARS AGO

TODAY

Remains of Organisms

Sand and Sediment

Trapped Gas

Trapped Oil

Natural gas, oil, and coal are all **fossil fuels**. They formed over millions of years. They come from the remains of plants and animals. These plants and animals lived millions of years ago. When they died, their remains **decomposed**. The remains were covered in water or earth. More plants and animals died. Their remains broke down and were covered. Many layers of buried remains formed. Over time, heat and pressure turned the remains into gas, oil, and coal. People must drill deep into the ground to get to fossil fuels. One day people could use up all of Earth's fossil fuels. It would take millions of years for more to form.

# CHAPTER THREE

# Renewable Energy

The second kind of energy source is renewable energy. This kind of energy does not run out. It is always there or can be easily replaced.

Solar energy is one example of this kind of energy. Solar energy comes from the sun. The sun heats Earth every day. Solar panels are made of materials that change sunlight into electricity. Some solar panels power homes. People put them on their roofs. There are also solar farms. Solar farms have many panels. They use giant mirrors to point sunlight toward the panels. These farms can power thousands of homes.

Solar farms have many solar panels to create electricity.

# How a Windmill Works

1. Blades Spin

2. Gear Spins the Generator

3. Generator Creates Electricity

4. Wires Carry Electricity

People can get energy from the wind. People build electric windmills the size of skyscrapers. The windmills are tall towers with blades that spin. The blades are shaped so that the wind will push them. The spinning of the blades turns a **generator** to create electricity.

Water power also uses movement to create electricity. This power comes from fast-moving water. The water may come from a large river. It could also come from water that falls through a dam. The water moves a through a turbine. This creates electricity.

Some power plants use Earth's heat to create electricity. Earth's core is very hot. It heats underground water. People drill deep wells. This brings hot water to the surface. People pump the water through turbines. The movement and heat create electricity.

Energy can come from plants and animal waste. People can burn wood to create heat. Crops can be burned as fuel. Power plants may burn food and yard waste to create electricity. Plant and animal waste can create a gas. This gas is called biogas. People can then burn biogas as fuel. Plants grow back. Animals will always create waste. So these are renewable sources.

People burn wood to create energy. The heat can be used for tasks such as cooking food.

Renewable energy is not always as reliable as nonrenewable energy. But it will always exist.

There will always be sun, wind, water, animals, and plants. But energy from these sources may not always be constant. The wind may stop blowing for a while. Or the sun could be covered with clouds. Batteries can store some energy for when this happens. Scientists are working to help them store more. Energy from fossil fuels is reliable. Nonrenewable sources give constant power. But unlike nonrenewable energy, renewable energy will always come back. It will never run out.

| Renewable vs. Nonrenewable Energy | |
| --- | --- |
| Does not run out | Runs out |
| Can be changed into electricity | Can be changed into electricity |
| Natural processes that renew | Takes millions of years to form |
| Renewable sources | Fossil fuels |

# Glossary

**decomposed** (dee-kom-POHZD) Something that decomposed has broken down into smaller pieces. Remains of plans and animals decomposed to form fossil fuels.

**electricity** (i-lek-TRISS-uh-tee) Electricity is a type of energy that can flow through wires. Electricity can come from many energy sources.

**fossil fuels** (FOSS-uhl FYOO-uhlz) Fossil fuels come from the remains of plants and animals that lived millions of years ago. Oil is a fossil fuel.

**generator** (JEN-ur-ay-tur) A generator is something that creates power. A windmill's generator spins to make electricity.

**nonrenewable** (non-ri-NOO-uh-buhl) Something that is nonrenewable cannot be replaced. Nonrenewable energy can run out.

**renewable** (ri-NOO-uh-buhl) Something that is renewable can be replaced by natural processes. Renewable energy does not run out.

**solar** (SOH-lur) Something that is solar has to do with the sun. Solar panels turn sunlight into electricity.

**turbine** (TUR-bine) A turbine is an engine that runs by the spinning of blades on a wheel. Steam, wind, and water can all power a turbine.

# To Learn More

## In the Library

Duling, Kaitlyn. *The Sun and Renewable Energy*.
New York, NY: Cavendish Square, 2020.

Howell, Izzi. *Energy*. New York, NY: Franklin Watts, 2019.

Vogel, Julia. *Discover Energy*. Mankato, MN: The Child's World, 2015.

## On the Web

Visit our website for links about renewable and
nonrenewable energy: **childsworld.com/links**

*Note to Parents, Teachers, and Librarians: We routinely verify our Web links to make sure
they are safe and active sites. So encourage your readers to check them out!*

# Index